Gallery Books
Editor: Peter Fallon

NONETHELESS

Peter Sirr

NONETHELESS

Gallery Books

Nonetheless
is first published
simultaneously in paperback
and in a clothbound edition
on 30 November 2004.

The Gallery Press
Loughcrew
Oldcastle
County Meath
Ireland

© Peter Sirr 2004

ISBN 1 85235 366 X (*paperback*)
    1 85235 367 8 (*clothbound*)

A CIP catalogue record for this book
is available from the British Library.

Contents

Irisch

Gib mir das Wegrecht
über die Kornstiege zu deinem Schlaf,
das Wegrecht
über den Schlafpfad,
das Recht, dass ich Torf stechen kann
am Herzhang,
morgen.

— Paul Celan (1920-1970)

Irish

Give me the right of way
over the corn steps into your sleep,
the right of way
over the steep path,
the right to cut peat
on the heart slope,
tomorrow.

— translated by Michael Hamburger

PART ONE

Settling

Now that the last box lies flattened against a wall
and everything hangs as if forever
we can learn to live here and not mind
that something keeps on moving,
something stays far away from us,

that sometimes we lie back
and nothing holds us, that concentratedly
a spider will cross the floor or absently
dust shift in its sleep, a draught wake a door knob;
that the house will have its quiet

in which nothing, and no one happens,
that all night it will pace, rearrange the furniture,
shake the photos from the albums, and enjoy
at last the sound of its own breath
gusting through the dark.

Orchard Music

Some residue of ourselves
shifts in the dust, presses against the air
to resist this life
                    or has come back
to wonder at it, to follow us
disbelievingly from room to room

How was it done, this thing?
Small accomplishments swell the air
almost with pain
the stir-fry sizzling in its pan
the table waiting

and at night
Sinatra to startle us as we sleep
our neighbour restless again
her own voice above it, high and thin

and glad. Why not something of that
lodged in the air, in the stereo's heart?

An infinity of incidents
took place, some of which
can no longer be remembered.

And the unseen lives went on
with sweet intensity: the sun rifling the empty house,
dust and spider lives, generations of furniture.

Greet them, wave to them as they pass
in and out, or stay

and the nothing human, the door
we never darkened;
an indifference, our lives unperceived

the never inhabited place, the air thickening with its
   branches . . .

Unbuilt

On my wall a print
of St Werburgh's Church,
white stone, solid spire —
too solid, as it happened,

too near the castle
for comfort, and so proscribed.
Nearby a dreamed-of street
comes out to play,

a giant cathedral
dips its toes in the river.
Monuments in every drawer:
the winged horses, the swords,

the upraised hands infinitely
persuading. Trams glitter among the trees,
their lacy, longed-for shelters
adorn the quays

and near the harbour,
in pavement cafés, their eyes shining,
the architects stay up all night
marching cities across a table.

In basement archives, patiently
the future carves its name,
the perfect avenues bide their time
just as, round every corner,

our own better lives catch fire.
Every now and then
we stumble on the plans
and marvel . . . Meanwhile, though,

there's this
dirt, mess, handsomeness,
the crooked streets persisting,
the sawn-off churches

keeping their peace, a grittiness
in the air like the breath
of the imagined, our
unfinished hearts

still building . . .

The Writer's Studio

(after the Francis Bacon Studio in the Municipal Gallery, Dublin)

They've been worrying for ages
how best to show your chaos.
Two days from the opening
a curator rearranges papers,
spills ink on the floor, half-eats an apple
and throws it in a corner, but still
the disorder comes to order;
the flung pipe, the forgotten shirt
sculpted and composed, with the notebooks,
the scrawled-on walls and mildewed postcards.
It's all there, through the peephole,
this reconstruction of your mind
from which you are entirely absent.
You're in heaven cursing the dullness of angels,
throwing your clothes around like clouds,
prowling the fragrant avenues
for a fight, a drink, someone to talk to
or sleep with, and if some freak wind
planted you here among your own things,
you'd sweep the lot from under our eyes,
tear it all down, rip the postcards, the T-shirts,
rob the till and drink it dry and float
back up to your high bed and wake up
having forgotten everything. We
who so loved your life we made a fetish of it
will stand in the air, hoping to catch
whatever falls: broken crockery, a smashed cloud,
we'll see your hand in the wind and rain,
hear your voice in the roaring streets,
follow you from porn shop to pub
and back again. And then a tree will fall,
or a leaf, someone lean out a window,

a cat slope
down a laneway
and
at last
we will understand you.

Office Hours

The workers disappear into their buildings,
the work itself falls through the air,
sinks into corners, remembers itself.
A notebook wakes up in a drawer;
in a forgotten diary, under mounds of clutter,
the umpteenth PAYE week of the year

is drawing to a close
as early lunch floats up from the restaurant
and rain pummels the fire escape.
Today's rain, last year's rain . . .
the door opens
and someone lumbers in

drenched in eighteenth-century rain,
the rain of the great squares, Luke Gardiner's rain,
the Earl of Drogheda's rain;
stands there shaking the rain from his cloak,
wanting his lunch,
then crosses the chessboard flagstones

and approaches us, a large, fretful
impatient gust.
But we're impatient too
and walk through him as through our own
scurrying selves that come towards us
with their stacks of paper and unmissable deadlines

and maybe one of them will stumble,
lift his head, stall
long enough to stare out a window
and sing our lost labours
in rooms for the never completed,
for the ongoing review, the unfinished application,

the meeting still searching for a conclusion.
The delicate letter weighs up its options,
the fax we have been waiting for
is coming through, the fax machine itself
is on the way
and though the diary's run out

and the taxes are paid
our working lives continue
in their own time, the cables are laid, the calls
are put through to our desks again,
our hands fallen into the air
nonetheless persist . . .

❖

This is where they came:
addressograph, adding machine,
adhesive tape dispenser, even the ashtray.

Smoke fills the office and no one
bats an eyelid, they're busy
with ballpoint pens, box-files and bulldog clips,

their thoughts are fixed on the slow clock,
the clack of coat hangers
and consequential loss, the costs

of carbon paper and calendars.
A clerk is searching in a drawer
from which in time will emerge

a double-hole punch and a dry-ink marker
while someone with a big desk
is speaking importantly into a dictaphone

and there's more to duty than drawing pins;
an invoice rots in a folder, unsuspected,
ungoverned, unforeseen, the list finder's

missing and the marginal lever
appears to be broken.
Someone reaches for paper clips,

someone is patiently removing staples
from a statement: here, at last,
is the single-hole punch,

a forest of treasury tags. All
here is shortfall, a feast of stolen
vetro-mobile files

and ghosts of effort disbelieving,
leaning against the Xerox
staring at a bundle

of discarded safety statements:
the trailing cables, the blocked
access/egress routes,

the broken chair
no one has yet rendered secure
pending disposal or repair,

here is the uneliminated spillage,
the unreported life, here
are sandwiches, flasks, a language

pressed against a window staring out
rubbing the steamed glass of the words
to see what else is there

In the Graveyard

They lived and died in the same place.
The same names occurring, same big skies above.
This close, they must move still in their cottages
and walk their fields, or stand now watching
the mountains purpling in the last sun
and hear the sea turning onto the slope of the beach
its calm, insistent weight. The air's crowded with them
as they move and watch and listen, no one
having told them otherwise. And if
absentmindedly they drift back here
to this silent field, they'll find
the gate locked before them and their names
unreadable on the stones. They'll walk back towards the
    village
and climb into their beds, whatever was theirs still theirs.

Strike

Hands blistered from his labour

Dublin Corporation
parks department, digging out stones

unsuited, untied, for uniform
an old shirt, a different paper

he comes home hot and angry,
sits down to dinner like someone
from the wrong life

the cutlery
lifted and weighed

where did *this*
come from?

He curses the work, eats with his new hands.

❖

I thought of him today as I cycled
head down through the fruit and vegetable market,
swerving to avoid trucks, the hoists
laden and scurrying like bumper cars,

still chewing a segment of radio news,
the clever young supervisor
with his Coketown brainwave,
a box of Pampers flourished on his table
to shame his workers from the toilet

the genius
of it

and later,
forkful of peas in my mouth, hurrying
from paper to book, avid for news.
The canteen lives in a permanent dark
of unbelief, everything except the food
has fallen off the planet. The teachers
are condemned, the train drivers
in their seventh week, the toll-booth operators
making noises. How difficult can it be
to take money from drivers? the newsman asks
in his newsman's voice. I push back the plate

transferred to the passenger seat
of a grey Ford Transit van my father is driving
through a '70s winter, the issue
still unresolved. The toys he delivered
persist in dreams . . . Some time later
he'll return to his suit and tie, his *Irish Times*,
to the mystery of his office in the city,

the cutlery will return, and the family faces
one by one

there will be
such clarity

but whenever I see him working

he's on strike, like now,
concentrating on the road and saying little,
painting lines or lugging stones
or forking hay in an ancient August

silent and thorough, as if this
is what he was born to do:
standing in the dusk in the heat of accomplishment . . .

❖

I lift my head
from the dim meal, from the twentieth page
of the funding application,
longing for hay, for a train to drive
or not to drive, longing to shrug,
down tools, make a placard and wave it
at myself

This labour persists
and if memory works its current of unrest
to bring out the dead
in protest, making him
come now through the gates
to stand in the day
with a list
of unreadable demands,
his clothes roughened
in preparation

the journey from my eye
to any one
of the papers on my desk
is all it takes to make him sway,
this thought, this second
is already the closing arbitration
that settles the issue, saves the industry,
sends him back through the gate
in his suit and tie, to his endless day.

Koblenz, Maybe

              Here
I have lived
maybe one minute in my mind
enough
for everything to be clear
furniture, morning light
                    dreams

agonies
of the possible

or, at last, the slow days unfolding
in the decided life

Haunted by this street
I walk
remembering another town
remembering you

our whole life spread before us
in that moment

and now returned
here

Here too the streets swell
with possible lives
and from each one
I lean out
drifting up

like the balloons over —
was it Koblenz? —
in their high quiet

On the motorway
now
a wicker basket on a trailer
speeding home

but in the field
the bubble descending
hands — mine, yours —
stretching for the ropes
and then
and now
in plunged silk
our bodies stilled

❖

oh why did I not
stay?

I climbed towards you
persistently, and you

you turned your face and leaned
all the way over, your voice

spilled into my mouth
No silence, true, that does not utter you

no blue no grey no rain no season
but you have ravaged

the light's thin curtain
and stitched my eyes to the fallen day

Home

Nearby, the crumbling palace;
nearby, the famous station
held up by fierce angels;

chewing gum clings
to the bus-park tarmac
like an old faith;

the ice-breaker *Strength*
waits for winter
at the end of the street;

someone puts his face in the sky
to suck a herring,
someone finds his wallet's gone;

at night the graveyards loosen,
the dead walk their streets again,
their mouths filled with names,

stones falling from their eyes;
and the routes oblige:
apartment buildings, hotels

crumble in their palms; a sigh
of concrete, sudden bones of steel,
the cleared ways tangled again,

coiling round repeatedly and always
an alley, a fencepost, a huckster's entrance
short of recognition; all night

the city multiplies; all night
sails out from itself and, bloated, returns,
each street its own harbour;

the dead walk their water;
from a quay wall I lean,
eyes sweeping the scene, as if

through glass, through water, through stone
something unshakeable might shine
and fix: the city disrobed, inviting;

milk-gleam of the known
street, the familiar house;
in the depths, in the deepest dark

of the innermost room a stillness
living and dead have drifted towards;
silent transaction, bones lent,

reconfigured, limbs tested, stretched,
sleep bartered with sleep,
the light, when it comes, changing hands.

The Tandem

The road began well, then faltered,
and like an idea whose time had not yet come
asphalt gave way to gravel
which finished in mud
but the ground was clear and sharp
like a mind woken to itself
      We're stitched together
in hedges and rain and open vistas
in the doorways of ruined houses behind trees
rust flowering in a graveyard of JCBs
and the barking of the perpetually alert
dogs of the region
      You slow the pedals, we lurch, almost fall
Slower now: take in everything, ride
softly over the earth. Down the slope
of a narrow road, past a city of caravans
and onto the beach
      You rush to embrace the sea
I push my face against the wire mesh
to study the caravans
a thesis growing
on productive confinement
infinite generations
sustained by bottled gas and poetry
and the spread calm of the bay
      You're out there inspecting the strandline
Bladderwrack, cabbage-kale, mermaid's purse
line up or don't, and perfect stones, and I hope
you'll look for me too
so we both can see
continually: everywhere the earth accumulates
and hums and enfolds and I am ashamed
to inhabit so little
      mysterious, long complex song
of the bird in the dunegrass behind me

a track
yet to be discovered
sitting in borrowed stillness
in the unlit dusk listening to banked cries
of the birds of the island, as outside
the sea pours its unhurried pleasure
       We lifted the bike and crossed over
a slender metal bridge
and reached a grassy bank beyond which
past deep pools and pocked
by a generation of rain
the road began again
We pedalled hard
       and here we are
a yellow house we fly to
ditch water and wild iris
the rusty unlikely tandem
freewheeling
devouring houses, hedges, trees
our motto Hunger, our time small
village and country, river and sea
       and sometimes surprised
into a kind of recognition
as if part of ourselves
lay scattered there
in patient, chanced vigil
and came now greeting
       drizzle hands, birdsong smile
body of fuchsia and stretched light
to welcome us

James Joyce Homeloans

At James Joyce's Bistro
James Dunne, proprietor and executive head chef
is to food what
but why not judge for yourself
the inner organs of beasts and fowl
or something a bit more conventional
10% off on presentation of this advert
and not a year goes by that doesn't see
in Adelaide the friends of Willunga and Adlinga
in Rome the ambassador
in Paris meanwhile a potluck picnic
in Fionn McCool's pub, Toronto
in Edwardian clothing
in Philadelphia the Potable Joyce
a watered-down version
in D'Arcy McGee's a singalong
while lemon soap in Sweny's
in Brazil, in Rio Grande do Sul
in the context of the celebration
of 25 years of the student bookshop
and always
in Trieste Zurich Buffalo Syracuse
in Jack Quin's Irish Ale House and Pub
saddle of rabbit with black pudding
lap of mutton
slab of luscious goosebosom
while in Sydney Harbour the *Ulysses* Challenge Yacht Race
and in Melbourne the oxen and the sperm
in the Domed Reading Room
there is no charge for the funeral
but bring a copy if you have one
and proudly supporting the festival
residential mortgages, remortgages

residential investment property or UK property finance
for all your mortgage needs
call us today or stop by!

Doktoro Esperanto

(L.L. Zamenhof 1859-1917)

Wherever he is the words are clear, swung back and forth
across the valleys. The mountains
have learned his language,
gods practise it and the woken come to it again

in a flurry of introductions. *Mi estas*
Doktoro Esperanto . . . No passports or signposts,
nothing flourished
or flagged; whoever is here has travelled far

and remembered
all sixteen unshakeable rules
of the Internacia Lingvo.
It leaps from their suitcases,

this language to stay up all night in.
The guns can't get through,
the earth articulate with graves
stays put

and he is back at his schoolboy desk
counting again
Unu, du, tri, kvar . . .
conscripting words from all the old armies,

scraping the uniforms off.
A world wakes in his notebook:
rooftop, sun, the streets of the city
wavering, shifting, then clear again, his hand

touching the table, the glass trembling *Bonvenon*!

'Here is everything . . .'

Here is everything
and you can't lose it

here the early morning sunlight archive
numbered, itemized, set down

the laundry rampant in its basket
here is the museum of bending down

here the breakfast gallery
halal grocer and rained pavement annals

bus ticket trove, the chronicle of standing
of the inhalation of perfume, of headlines

urgencies of the mobile phone
eternally held, no thought erased

breath unexamined, no hair unturned, bone
unpicked

labyrinths of the least machine
here you are

locked forever
in the Museum of Soviet Calculators

websites of forgotten code
everything

somewhere
its own monument: and already

they arrive
the whitecoated, loving curators

the visitors filing past
to wonder and be wondered at

'Cobalt door, yellow walls . . .'

Cobalt door, yellow walls
wooden frame where the name will go
though still no name appears, the shelves are bare
this halal temple grocer spicery
sells winter and nervousness to the waiting street.
Next door in the off-licence I buy my paper
from where the beans used to be, find
the wine has moved, the coffee shifted, the counter
is repositioned. They're ready for anything
though still no one comes.
It may never open, it may be
the deal's fallen through, the tenant run away
to Sark, to Lundy, to Sikkim,

exactly now he is unrolling his blind
and selling his first umbrella of the day
while here people are travelling for miles
to come away with one hand
as long as the other, to enjoy the unfilled shelves
and conjure names into the wooden frame.
It could be theirs, this blue and yellow beacon,
this fading radio station whose signal
keeps sending us home
to change our lives, to move tables, chairs
and sit on the floor in a great
cleared space imagining the shelves
of Athos, Punial, Andorra . . .

'Out of a dream of argument . . .'

Out of a dream of argument
you come to me, waving
all your minds, feeding dark with dark,
the air with thunder, throwing up your arms to form
the milky flashes someone steers by: *Harm's
Way, The Broken Bow* . . .

The moon shows, white hole
through which ease slipped.
Something heavy, stupid
is labouring to pursue, there's
the too near clump of boots,
my body flattening the grass

of a hollow — all of which
put down to the mind's slowness,
its obtuseness in sorrow to delay,
to lie low and then, wittily, to remember.
Grandly it flashes now: the limbs
twitch, the images pulse, the hollow's

stumbled into. I wake to inquisition
and the ebb of your body,
the miracle of your life elsewhere —
as if, in this morning fire of separation,
your hand had only now descended
and reached in to pick the bone . . .

'Such clarity: how . . .'

Such clarity: how
the wind blows,
the economy shrinks, disgrace

is everywhere; someone phones in, excited, it's
the young, the old,
foreigners with their hands stretched out;

today
the cloned sheep is older than her years,
arthritis flowering in her borrowed bones,

and the politician in his surprising cell
is issued the standard ration
of eggs, hash browns, toast and tea.

How many sugars? Milk or black?
His faithful driver answers a hunger,
gives us two fingers through the window

and takes off at speed; today
knows this
and takes equally in its stride

the archaeology of the toothbrush: lost
cities thrive on a bristle
and lie in wait; and still to come

the postman gunned down, the hurricane
gravely climbing the ratings,
the groomed voice

high above the tangled city
which tells us
repeatedly we're stuck, we're standing still,

the world announced all round us, the air
heavy with answers; today's
going nowhere

and not listening, today feels
at the light's edge
something stir, slow burn, today's

no one, the guest
without argument, speechless in the studio,
nothing but a sweet blankness lodged in the bone.

'A new geography: how . . .'

A new geography: how
lately I have begun to travel your body
with a kind of carelessness, knowing
the journey is repeatable,

to look at you without hurry
knowing you'll be there
at the end of it, the rainbow
at the end of the rainbow, gently

persisting.
Intently we burrow into one another
and come back whole, to the calm night, fur
in our mouths, bone on the tongue, resting.

'We will make a pit, then . . .'

We will make a pit, then
put her in it and then we shall all throw
stones. The exact size yet to be specified
and indeed it may yet be decided
to tie her to a tree instead. It will be
whatever we all have agreed, the law
is quite flexible on this point.
At no particular time the back of the lorry
flips down and the shooting begins.
There are always hands to be tied, details
to be arranged. The football stadium
is not ideal, but it's all we have. Give us money
for a killing ground and we'll kill them there.
At dusk they bring them out and kneel them down
in the penalty box, at noon the fire is lit,
throughout the night the hanging truck
tours the villages, at dawn the boy wakes up
who later with his pals will take the girl out to the woods,
pinning the crime in schoolboy script
to her frayed sweater.

'We stepped out of our skins . . .'

We stepped out of our skins
into the train, descended to walk
like astronauts on the soft sand —

what dull planet had we landed from,
grey, exhausted? —
receiving the day with open arms.

We listened to each other and simultaneously
to the sea's plans, the gulls' forecasts.
Above us

a man dangled from the air
in a purple parachute, caught between suburb and sea,
hardly moving

then came down slowly —
helmet, orange suit, heavy boots —
his legs barely bending.

We moved off, shy of the business,
the pulled chute, tangle of cords,
the soft burden hauled towards the grass.

We made for the hilltop
and kept on going, undecided
between Killiney and Wales.

What words we brought
have fallen down
and no one now will hear from us.

All we can transmit is a planet
unexpectedly light
and our hands rushing to open it.

A lovely hesitation holds us.

'Sail out from your harbour . . .'

Sail out from your harbour.
Be my ambassador as I'll be yours
though silent, without credentials
and reporting nothing. Your voice pours in

the sea, the sun, every day's
destination. You arrive late
in the unmapped town, and no one there
or everyone, and everything

beheld and remembered. The notebooks fill: how
the new boots grip and I miss
the picture, lying back in a darkened room.
Light, sail into me

but very slowly, the clouds come down
in their own time. From the heights,
the precipices, your voice, last night's
fire round which a whole world gathered

but this is it too, and I'm in it
and like it. Shall I FedEx
a passing car, the radio left on downstairs?
Or today's mission for supplies

to the same few streets but altered
continually? It's as if
the disk crashed, with nothing saved
and every day begins with the crank

of promising machinery: slow boot-up,
aches and buzzings giving way
to a blue silence. I can send
the date, the time, the objects considered each in its turn,

the silence that sits like a mountain
between me and the door, and the pleasure
of the slow climb over: the noise, the expectation,
the city waiting like a liner . . .

'A book with the names of the hanged . . .'

A book with the names of the hanged
their names in columns, lightly travelled

certain bodies borne off to the prosecutor's door
or dragged by Volunteers to the waiting professors

the urban renewal of the call
to have the deed brought back from behind the wall

where, for good order, they had placed it
And it was granted, again

colourful scenes on the green, in the square
this one strangled and thrown upon the pyre

this one and his brother strung up yesterday
a harvest, recently, of botched bones

where the inexpertly hacked still lay
deep in the city   and today

alerted by radio to the buzzing of cranes
slowly winching the five victims up

'God is great!', the cranes mounted
on the backs of trucks, someone's

glad thought   always this   always those at the back
with toddlers, straining for a better look

from bathroom to breakfast
a thin span of rage, then . . .

a building crew waits
for the return of the cranes

a rope holds, a crowd
disperses, gathers again

'Somewhere the mild...'

Somewhere the mild
unassembled cities
the gods let slip,

empires we won't be queuing for,
public health projects
and planning laws,

the farmers in their fields again
sowing the seeds of oblivion.
Here, though,

every bulletin brings us
the eagle-man, obsidian, the flayed god
and his strange people;

here the drugged boy stares out
mad-eyed from the poster,
temples glare

and as always the knife
'is delicately inlaid
with turquoise and mother-of-pearl'.

Somewhere the quiet life
un-gaped at, its pots and pans,
billhooks and receipts

but here the gods wake up hungry,
everyone's hungry
or hungered for

and *when the dawn came*
then they made them leave
that they might go to die

for during the entire festival
they were all flayed
and those captives who had died

they called the eagle-men . . .

Somewhere the museum
of trash TV, forgotten dinners
and the yard swept clean again

somewhere the vast spaces
where for hours we linger
over histories of air and water

where we listen
to the lost in their snug valleys sending forth
nothing whatsoever

'I rest my head in the barber's hands . . .'

I rest my head in the barber's hands
I rest my body in the winter light
and saunter
past gambling club, milkbar, manicurist
and stuck-up *enoteca*
stopping as always to watch
a bow window erupt from the corner
misshapen, haphazard
as if the hole had just been gouged out
and the thing fitted
and yet
a strange delicacy about it

Another hole punched through time
by the entrance of the forgotten park
the keeper's lodge
that's drifted in from somewhere else,
planet
of light-answering brick, of gothic childhoods,
some slow creature climbing to my shoulder
to sit and stare, who has no need
to travel any farther than this,
whose life rests
on a single brick
printed with branch light.
It fades and gathers, the garden waits
and nothing, me least of all
can move

At the edge of the mind
a ring of slow trees,
municipal water's
reliable roar
and beyond that the hum of memory,

the trillion details building
their alien city
on the other side of this
green, stalled, bricked-up
moment, this light's
edition, this
bubble blown from a morning,
early January, three streets from home
and somehow holding

'In early and in latter rain . . .'

In early and in latter rain
to be there
and not perish
the grass
with'reth
and the flower thereof
blessed are they
blessed are the dead
and the waiting husbandman
the heaped riches
of the cathedral air
of our bodies lost in this
the music opens a giant crack
and we leap in
for a little while
labour and sorrow
and now
swallowed, winged, gladdened
surely all our days
surely some joy
unconstrained
come to rest
in the continuing place

The Leavetaking of the Ceremonious Traveller

'Congedo del viaggiatore ceremonioso' by Giorgio Caproni

Friends, I think it best
that I should now begin
taking down my suitcase.
Even if I don't know exactly
the time of arrival, nor what stations
come before mine, certain signs
inform me, reaching my ears
from the places hereabout,
that I shall have to leave you soon.

Kindly excuse me
the slight disturbance I cause.
I have been happy among you
since we left, and am much
in your debt, believe me,
for your excellent company.

I would love to spend more time
conversing with you. But that's the way.
Where I'm supposed to catch the connection
I have no idea. I feel however
that I shall often recall you,
transplanted to my new seat,
while already my eye sees from the window,
beyond the damp smoke of the large cloud
approaching us, the red disk of my station.

I take my leave of you
without being able to conceal
a slight frustration.
It was so pleasant to talk

amongst ourselves, sitting opposite
each other, to mingle faces (smoking,
exchanging cigarettes)
and all our tale-telling
(the easy way we can tell others)
even to be able to confess
things which, even if pressed
(mistakenly) we'd never dare reveal.

(Pardon me. It's a heavy case
even if there's not much in it.
I wonder indeed why I bothered
bringing it, and what possible use
it will be to me. But all the same
I have to carry it, if only from habit.
Excuse me please. There we are.
Now that it's in the corridor
I feel freer. Please excuse me.)

I was saying how nice it was
to be together, chatting away.
We've had such disputes,
it's only natural,
and nearly come to blows —
what could be more normal? —
more than once, only courtesy
restraining us. However that may be
I want to thank you all again,
and from the bottom of my heart,
for your marvellous company.

I take my leave of you, doctor,
and of your eloquent doctrine.
Farewell, slender little girl, your face
so gently coloured, that whiff

of playground and meadow . . .
Goodbye, soldier
(O sailor! On earth
as in heaven and at sea).
Farewell peace and war
and to you, Father,
who asked me (in all jest)
if I had it in me to believe
in the *true* God.

Farewell to knowledge
and farewell to love.
Farewell too to religion.
It seems I've arrived.
Now that I can hear the brake
more vigorously applied
I leave you finally, dear friends.
Farewell. Of one thing I'm certain,
that I have reached a calm
desperation, undismayed.

I'm getting off. Enjoy the rest of your journey.

Nonetheless

I thought of you this morning
as I walked across the beach

through spring, summer, spring again
and deadly winter

fistfuls of iced wind
followed by two rainbows

waltzing across the bay
wanting the word for all of it

as for the hour spent reading the waves
with my back against the buttress

of the ruined abbey crowded with graves
as a shadow moved across the mountain

like a god mopping his brow
and the rain gathered its thoughts again

the grey cathedral islands darkening
meanwhile in the distance

and remembering
the verb you sent me last winter

for feeling low in a new place
as the winds howl and the inhabitants

keep their distance
and which I stored with the others

the one for falling down a well
unknowingly

the one for waking
in a panic of loss

three February mornings
in a row

the one for rain on the mountain
finally entering the soul

as, nearby, a wolf sniffs
ancient urine

the one for living
in the endless

promise of language
while all around the world swells

with avid grammars
and hardly a thing that happens

survives our greedy mouths
Nonetheless, you say

nonetheless
asusu, egthu, gobray

to love for the last time
to carry a feather on your back

along the road
lit by rushes and a slow

avenue of trees, the silence of it
to plunge

through the grounds of the house and out
along the grass path to the beach

running with you
through spring, summer, spring again

and deadly winter
to walk to sleep with a wounded knee

backwards, while chanting
the thousand words for *know*

nonetheless . . .

PART TWO

Edge Songs

i

Eyes up from the page to behold
silence, locked sky, hear the lake
lapping, deep and grey, the solitary blackbird
in its tree: hurry! all of these now
the quick impulse of it, slantwise
scribbled on the edge of the moment
this hasty space, trembling margin
this at last a place to live in

ii

The Irishman wants meat and drink.
The air stirs, the god lies quiet
in his room

silence, work, the rule
that we may be sustained without harm
regaling the body poorly, advancing daily

but stop here
where the crops ripen
and the vines swell
the sea the earth
even the stars fatten

move then,
fly to the bishop, tell him
his servant is dry
tell him
we shall survive our sustenance

iii

The forest sang to me
when I was with Cuirithir
and the sea sang to me

he was my

Cuirithir the ex-poet, the
otter-footed
where is he?

south of the wooden chapel
lies the stone
where we used to meet

every evening I drift there
after the triumph of prayer

a blast of flame
           how shall I

he will have nothing
the ex-poet

iv

From innumerable instances
a wonderful supply of butter
a wonderful supply of pork
her crops remain dry in the rain
she hangs her cloak on a sunbeam
turns water to beer

she causes a foetus to disappear
makes salt from rock
her mantle is not stained by raw meat
a river rises up against cattle thieves
wolves are her swineherds
and wild ducks come to her
a band of murderers is deceived
by a miracle of glamour
she cures a man of overeating
the miraculous transport of a large tree
she moves a river
she divines honey
and even after her death
the millstones will not grind a pagan's corn
pray for me who am worthy of blame
here ends the life of Brigid the virgin

v

Here among Carinthian boors
a forest of shut doors

give me
the wood of Allabair and Argatbran

the mist skittering
across the headland

the company of old friends

vi

The cold trees cage the air

what was it

every dribble a swollen river
every ford a full lake
every lake a sea
the horses stuck, the hungry deer
ice fills the eagle's mouth
the fish of Ireland on the move
wide-eyed in Cuan, in Key Wood
conversing with wolves, blackbirds
not a strand the waves don't hammer
not a badger left, nor a path

better off in quilt and feathers
as long as ice holds the fords

in cold Moylurg . . .

vii

The north wind blows, there's snow in the air
everything lurches and shudders
the earth itself sickens in fear
the sea flounders and hard stones groan
the north wind shakes its axe and roars
oaks dance like reeds
the sun creeps back to its shelter
we three scholars, priests
tossed and torn

oppressed by weather
marvellous Hartgar
consider our weariness
aid us your Irish scholars
and thereby climb
to the temples of heaven

     viii

Last night Christ the Sun rose from the dark
harvesting himself from the fields of God
and now the wandering tribes of bees
are spilled in scarlet flowers, now the winds
are soft with birds, the churches huge
with halleluias: take it, father, yours by right
this Easter joy, threshold of the light

     ix

These
delicately arrayed lights,
the latest art,
your multi-coloured dome,
every room a garden
of unkillable blooms —
however the wind blows
they'll never know

We on the other hand
live in perpetual gloom
our walls bare, our doors unlocked
the ceiling black with soot.

Give thanks to Neptune, whose dark showers
have found us out.
Blow, blow, east wind, once more
and the walls are finished.

Vulcan's brat, Cacus,
you'd like it here
a labyrinth minus light or joy,
the house shivers in its black cloak,
when daylight comes we send it back
not known at this address.

Heaven for moles or bats
though hardly fit
for the likes of us
I think you'll agree.
My lord, why not
bring everything to me that cannot see,
let me be the saintly warden
stumbling round
your Asylum for the Blind

or, great father, all wise
clap your hands, give the nod
to the builder and his men,
throw some light on us your servants
give us shiny locks and keys
and windows to spill the sun
on scholars' bones, let warmed hearts
love, my lord, continually
the light and sun and you

X

What else should we swear on, if not the earth
how should we walk, if not so lightly
we hardly touched it

yesterday's laughter, yesterday's wine
are nothing now, the bones of the sun
are dust already

so wrap your arms around fallen water
hold on tight to joy, to whatever
slips through your fingers

where else can the world go
but away from us, like an ebbing tide
and what should we do

but follow

xi

Rejoice, the Northmen bleed
the horde of braggarts
Christ has undone them
thirty thousand gloriously slaughtered
not counting the menials
lord of the world
Christ the magnificent
our tower and shield, Hosanna

xii

Forever cold, my curse on wind, my curse on water
raindrops big as fists, snowflakes like sheep
forever cold, forever numbness
bare bones on a bare table
the frost has closed the roads
ice in the mouth, ice in the veins
forever cold, forever winter
sewing in our mouths its shroud of prayer

xiii

oh why did I not
stay?

I climbed towards you
persistently, and you

you turned your face and leaned
all the way over, your voice

spilled into my mouth
No silence, true, that does not utter you

no blue no grey no rain no season
but you have ravaged

the light's thin curtain
and stitched my eyes to the fallen day

xiv

White body, bluegrey eyes

between his throat and face
a branch of red berries

Fróech crossing the dark water

if I live forever
I will not see anything as beautiful

xv

Honeybag
son of juice, son of lard
floating
on buttermilk and curds

leek and bacon
and full-fat butter
kidney, rib, shoulder
welcome to your land

the fish of Inver Indsén
dance for you
cabbage curls for you
unceasing cheese

and sheep's milk porridge
whatever you have eaten
risen again
and waiting: loin, leg,

breastbone
the gravy returns to the pot
geese flock from your gullet
and briefly circle the island

before flying back
ready roasted to your plate
what is ther in Paradis
cloved and cinnamoned

the larks drop down
Bot grasse and flure and grene ris
the place so generous
you'll die of it, and still eat

      xvi

Stay back, don't come near
my mind's not on you
it still roams
the battleblood of Féic

my bloody body lies beside
Leitir Dá mBruach
my unwashed head
you carried here

arrogance to make a tryst
that ignores the death tryst
sad journey, fore-ordained
my grave marked out on Féic

lost
in a blaze of desire

carry me gently now

my fine war-band
did not betray me
grey-horsed, joyous
they sang to the end

the green-leafed forest
has received them

don't come near
my mind's not on you

my five-pointed spear
my five-circled shield
and the oaths sworn on it

my chessboard is yours, blood
stains its edge, it is not far away

the bitch Morrigu is among us
unwelcome guest
who hurls us to battle

she washes the spoils
her hair thown back
her laughter cold

the heart in my dead body hates her

go on your way

let us part now
while parting is fair

don't wait here

everything I've known
I'll leave with my men
in the morning light
someone will remember my song

remember this

see that the stone is strong
and well dug-in

my wrecked body will leave you
the death god torture my soul

let my words remain

my love
don't speak to me

xvii

What
consolation there?

Fothad Canainne
killed at Féic
lover of the wife
of Ailill Flann Bec

I would find your stone
look for her
grieving figure

know her name

xviii

I read, I write, I study
eat, drink a little, sleep
and pray

I would do more

reach out from the narrow room
to throw a little fire into the world

and watch over it
all the days of my life

until it blazed

xix

Winter is cold, the wind has risen

the stags are listening
to wolfmusic

I, Caílte, and brownhaired Diarmait
and lightfooted Oscar
at the end of a cold night
listened to wolfmusic

Today I'm an old man
and recognize few

but how proudly I would shake my spear
on ice-cold mornings

I softened the cough of armies
and thank the king of heaven
son of the virgin
though tonight I am very cold

xx

Since I can see, every day,
the ropes loosening,
and huge hurry in your eyes,
since this place has drifted off
already, and the work we've shared
is a receding island
I give in to your journey home.
Who could refuse a lover?
And how could I argue with you
since the journey's mine too
or would be, if Christ gave me back
my time again, my old strength.
My friend, forgive me my dotage
and listen to the poet's message
'Time bears everything away,
including memory . . . '
The blood dulls and chills,
our strength fades and the heart
shrinks: how they terrify now,
the sea-routes, the jagged coasts.
I will stay
on our vanished island
and find a beam

to hang my days on, my eyes
will not look back.
But you mustn't delay,
sail away swiftly,
and remember your friend.
Remember the world passes
like the wind, is carried off
like smoke into the empty air.
God grant you safe passage
to the coasts of Ireland,
may you be happy and famous,
may you pluck joy from this life
and be rewarded in the next . . .

xxi

A hard winter but now
things are on the move again
one foot shifts in front of the other
and the little Iranian bakery
is open, flat bread and cakes
for lunch, a large bird
holed up in the blossomy tree
three cats stretched on the extension roof

that have strayed out somehow from the book
to prove a point: winter's gone
and three kinds of spring have returned
three groggy heads lift up
from the complicated morning
to stare at the view, three suns
shift in the sky like old friends
Hello Hello Hello

and we'll go roving again
by the banks of the three rivers
we'll fall down each night
in the three dark places of Ireland
forgive me if I rest my head
on the pillow of Knowth
while you stretch out in Slaney
the dawn will find us wrapped together

in the cave of Ferns, and
washed by three waterfalls
in Clonmacnois, in Clones, in Clonard
we'll raise our triplicate hymn
we'll sing sing sing
of the three holidays of the landless man
three things which justice demands
three rejoicings followed by sorrow

my love, three kinds of cake
are left in the bakery
and all have cream, there is
all manner of sweetness in Taybah
and knowledge floods the room
it shines on your face your aspect your speech
the three sparks that kindle love
are all blazing

Notes and Acknowledgements

'Edge Songs' (pp 61-76) is a series of workings, adaptations, versions, 'skeleton' translations of poems in Old Irish, Middle Irish and Latin, as they might be remembered or misremembered by an imagined Irish poet, and sometimes original poems written in response to or in the shadow of poems from that tradition.

iii   Based on ninth-century Irish poems of the love of Líadan and Cuirithir preserved in two sixteenth-century mss. See for example Gerard Murphy, *Early Irish Lyrics: Eighth to Twelfth Century* (Oxford: Clarendon Press, 1956), pp 82-85.

iv   This poem is composed from the section titles in Liam de Paor's translation of *The Life of Brigid the Virgin* from the seventh-century Latin of Cogitosus in *Saint Patrick's World* (Four Courts Press, 1993).

vi   This poem 'remembers' the famous 'Fuit, fuit!/Fuar a-nocht Magh leathan Luirg' written near Roscommon in the tenth- or eleventh-century.

vii-ix   Versions of the ninth-century Sedulius Scottus, one of the most brilliant Latin poets of his period. viii adapts Helen Waddell's translation in *Medieval Latin Lyrics* (Constable, 1930). Six of Scottus's poems are reproduced and translated in Peter Godman, *Poetry of the Carolingian Renaissance* (Duckworth,1985).

x   Response to a poem, 'Ná luig, ná luig', probably eleventh-century, reproduced in James Carney, *Medieval Irish Lyrics* (Dolmen, 1967).

xi   A 'micro-translation' of a long poem by Sedulius Scottus.

xiv   See 'Athesc Findabrach', 'Findabair Remembers Fróech' in Carney, page 90. The lines are from the eighth-century *Táin Bó Fraích*.

xv   Conflates lines from 'Aisling Mhic Chonglinne' (eleventh- or twelfth-century) and 'The Land of Cockaigne' (early fourteenth-century) from The Kildare Book.

xvi   Version of poem written c. 900. See David Greene and Frank O'Connor (eds) *A Golden Treasury of Irish Poetry A.D. 600 to 1200* (Macmillan, 1967).

xviii Adapts a poem by Sedulius Scottus.
  xix From the twelfth-century Irish. See 'Description of
       Winter and Memory of the Past' in Gerard Murphy,
       page 51.
   xx Version of 'Colman's Farewell to Colman', ninth-
       century Latin, reproduced and translated in Peter
       Godman, pp 280-281.

Acknowledgement is due to the following publications where
some of these poems, or versions of them, first appeared: *Free
Verse, The Irish Times, The Journal of Irish Studies* (Tokyo),
Metre, Poetry Daily, Poetry Ireland Review and *The Stinging
Fly.*
   The author acknowledges also the assistance of a bursary
from An Chomhairle Ealaíon / The Arts Council, Ireland, in
the completion of this collection.

The epigraph, from *Fadensonnen: Gedichte* by Paul Celan
(Suhrkamp Verlag, Frankfurt am Main, 1968) and *Poems of Paul
Celan*, translated by Michael Hamburger (Anvil Press, London,
and Persea Books, New York, 1995), is reproduced by kind
permission of the publishers.